1) Draw thirteen small lowercase a's.

2) Put a big a around them and two small a's above them.

3) Attach a V, two d's and two b's.

4) Make four radioactive squiggles and thirteen green eyes.

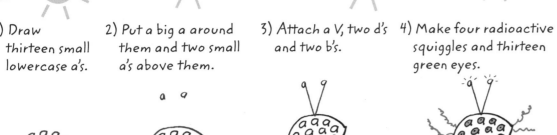

DRAW AN ALIEN

Good morning from the Andromeda Galaxy!

I've traveled 2,500,000 light years just to check out what's going on in your Milky Way.

Astronomers think that our two galaxies are going to collide in a few billion years.

DRAW A BABOON

No *time to eat?* If a baboon senses danger while gathering food, it will stuff a whole meal into its cheeks. Then it can either eat on the run or find a safe place to dine in peace.

1) Draw a long b.

2) Add a c and two short lines.

3) Draw three curves, seven lines, and a pair of eyes.

4) Make four squiggly curves, one smooth curve, and a squared curlicue.

5) Attach a squiggly curlicue and an S.

6) Add loopy hands and feet.

There's a B in this lady's bonnet!

1) Draw a curvy C.

2) Attach a wide curvy C.

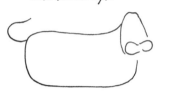

3) Add three more C's, one backwards and one sideways.

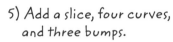

4) Draw two loopy ears, two O's, two curlicues, and a curve.

5) Add a slice, four curves, and three bumps.

6) Draw three legs and four wedge hooves.

7) Make black splotches and green grass.

DRAW A COW

Have a cow by drinking milk at breakfast, lunch, and dinner. There are millions of Holstein dairy cows, and each one has a completely different black and white pattern.

Check out these two crazy cows:

Cash Cow

Alpha Cow

1) Draw a D lying down.

2) Put an i on top.

3) Add a squiggle between three straight lines...

4) on top of a triangle...

5) on top of five bars...

6) on top of a trapezoid.

7) Add a roof, walls...

8) and twenty yellow windows.

DRAW A DOME

You used a capital D to draw this dome. Where could you find a real dome? On top of the United States Capitol, which is in Washington, D.C., our nation's capital.

1) Draw two e's.

2) Attach three V's...

3) and two more V's, upside down.

4) Add three curls and two curly V's.

5) Draw loopy hands...

6) eyes, mouth, stripes, hair, and suspenders.

DRAW AN ELF

Pointy-eared mischievous creatures, elves can be found in meadows, myths, and the North Pole.

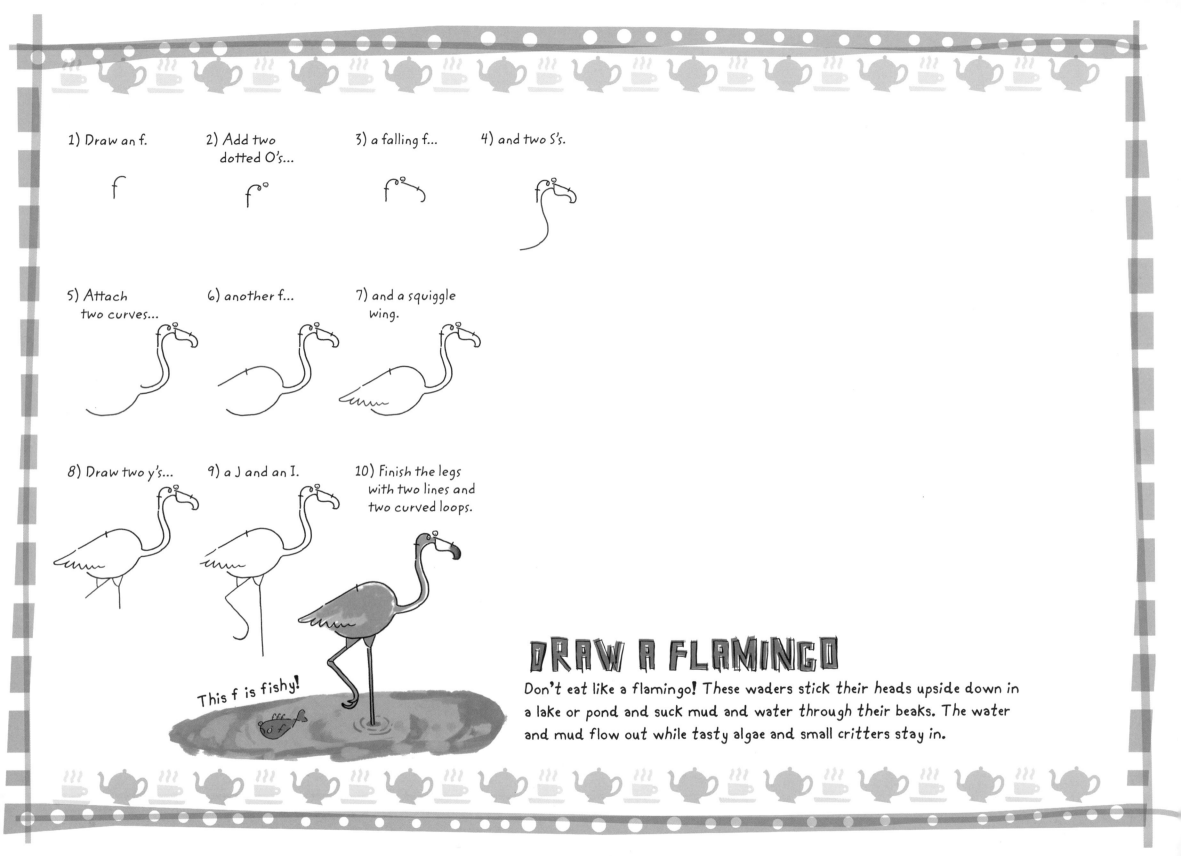

1) Draw an f.

2) Add two dotted O's...

3) a falling f...

4) and two S's.

5) Attach two curves...

6) another f...

7) and a squiggle wing.

8) Draw two y's...

9) a J and an I.

10) Finish the legs with two lines and two curved loops.

This f is fishy!

DRAW A FLAMINGO

Don't eat like a flamingo! These waders stick their heads upside down in a lake or pond and suck mud and water through their beaks. The water and mud flow out while tasty algae and small critters stay in.

1) Draw a long g.

2) Add a half ziggy line...

3) a small c, and a dotted i.

4) Attach a big speckled bean.

5) Draw a teardrop ear and tail...

6) three sideways waves...

7) a skinny W...

8) four wedged hooves and more speckles.

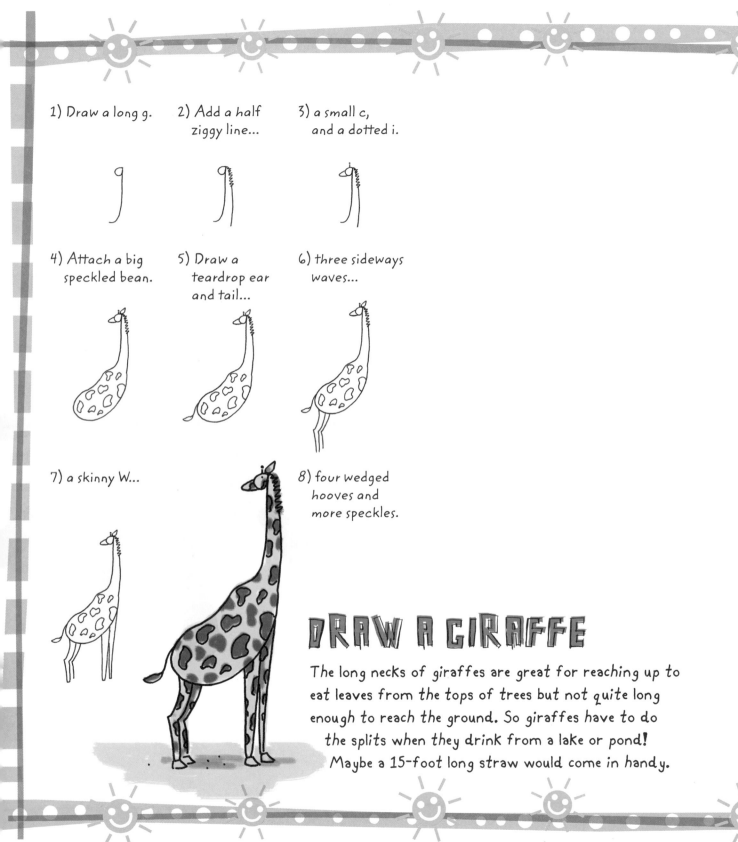

DRAW A GIRAFFE

The long necks of giraffes are great for reaching up to eat leaves from the tops of trees but not quite long enough to reach the ground. So giraffes have to do the splits when they drink from a lake or pond! Maybe a 15-foot long straw would come in handy.

1) Draw a swoopy h.

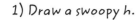

2) Attach two curves.

3) Add one long squiggly line and two shorter squiggly lines.

4) Draw two h's...

5) and connect with three curves.

6) Draw eight curvy curves...

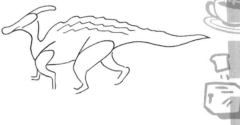

7) and attach loopy paws.

8) Choose your own colors since no one really knows what color dinosaurs were.

DRAW A HADROSAUR

What dinosaur looked like a duck, acted like a cow, and played the tuba? The hadrosaur! Hadrosaurs had duck-billed snouts and roamed the earth in herds over 65 milllion years ago. Some hadrosaurs had hollow crests on top of their heads that scientists think might have been used to make sounds like a tuba.

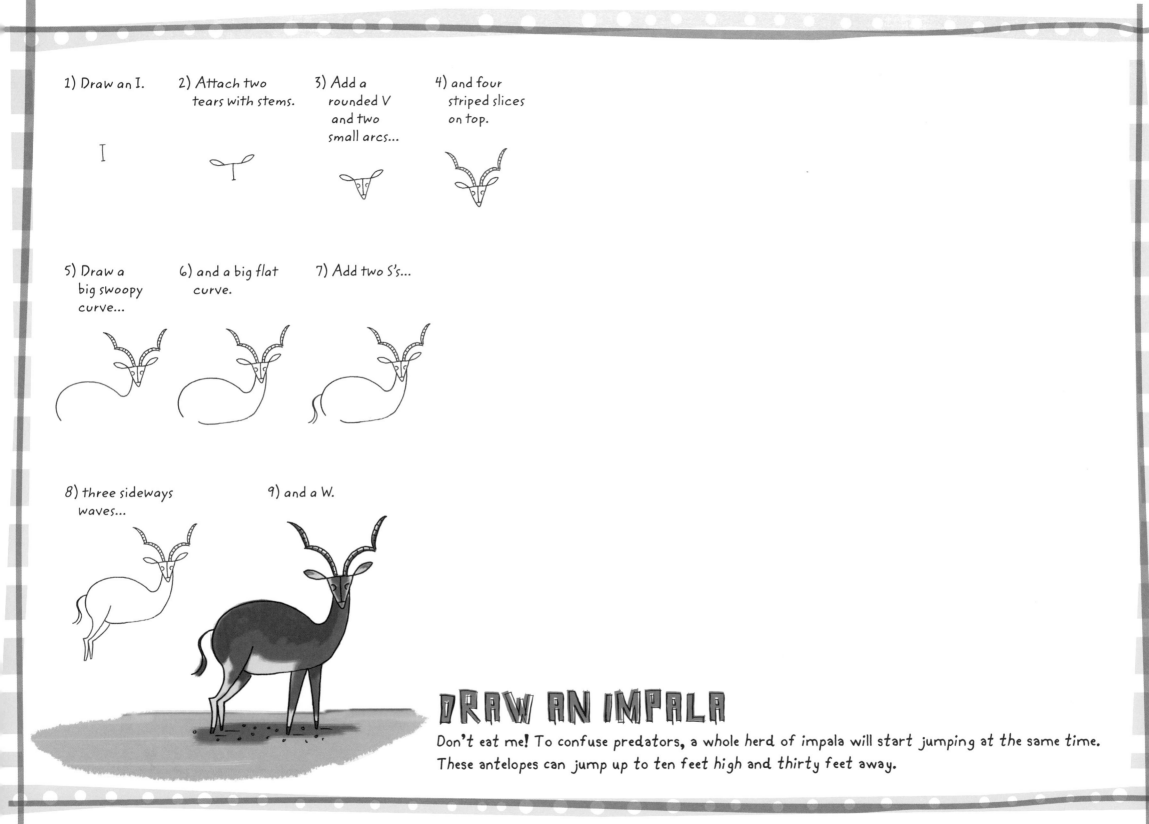

1) Draw an I.

I

2) Attach two tears with stems.

3) Add a rounded V and two small arcs...

4) and four striped slices on top.

5) Draw a big swoopy curve...

6) and a big flat curve.

7) Add two S's...

8) three sideways waves...

9) and a W.

DRAW AN IMPALA

Don't eat me! To confuse predators, a whole herd of impala will start jumping at the same time. These antelopes can jump up to ten feet high and thirty feet away.

1) Draw a striped J.

2) Connect two more J's.

3) Add a backwards question mark...

4) a striped C and...

5) connect them to the J's.

6) Add a b and d on top...

7) a W on the bottom and...

8) four striped curls, on top and bottom.

9) Give your juggler eleven spinning plates and a steady eye.

DRAW A JUGGLER

Don't try this at breakfast—it's hard to eat from a spinning plate! People have been juggling plates, balls, clubs, knives, and torches for thousands of years, just for fun.

1) Draw a k.
2) Attach a triangle...
3) and a curlicue...

4) a C with curlicues...
5) two triangles...
6) and four V's.

7) Give the knight a lance...
8) and a horse.

DRAW A KNIGHT

The medieval knight was like a tank—protected from head to toe in a suit of armor, heavily armed, and riding high on horsepower.

1) Draw two l's.

2) Add two sideways cursive l's.

3) Draw two rounded loops down and four pointed loops up.

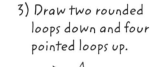

4) Add eight upside-down V's...

5) and two curvy M's.

6) Put a V around the bottom...

7) a squiggly C around that, and a little c in the middle.

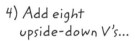

DRAW A LOTUS

The lotus flower rises bright and beautiful out of the muddy bottom of ponds. Every part of the plant can be eaten, including the seed pod that grows in the flower's center.

1) Draw an M.

2) Connect the ends with a smile.

3) Add two palm trees...

4) an O with teeth...

5) two beady eyes...

6) blue fur...

7) and running feet!

DRAW A MONSTER

Dangerous, terrifying, hideous, or just misunderstood? Monsters are not like me and you, so NEVER ask a monster what he ate for breakfast.

1) Draw an N.

2) Add a very skinny striped triangle.

3) Attach a big swoop...

4) and a big curve.

5) Draw three tears...

6) and lots of gray blobs.

DRAW A NARWHALE

The narwhale lives in the Arctic Circle. It uses its long tusk to poke through thin ice so that it can breathe.

1) Draw two small, dotted O's.

2) Add a tiny triangle, curve, and angle.

3) Make two pointed ears connected by three curves.

4) Draw four rows of splotchy spots...

5) with a big hook curve on top.

6) Make two curvy loops...

7) and connect with a curve.

8) Draw two loopy legs and a loopy tail.

9) Add more spots and put your ocelot in a tree.

DRAW AN OCELOT

Can you spot this cat? The ocelot hides in trees and brush so it can ambush its prey. Its spots look like black and brown blobs and doughnuts that connect in places to make stripes.

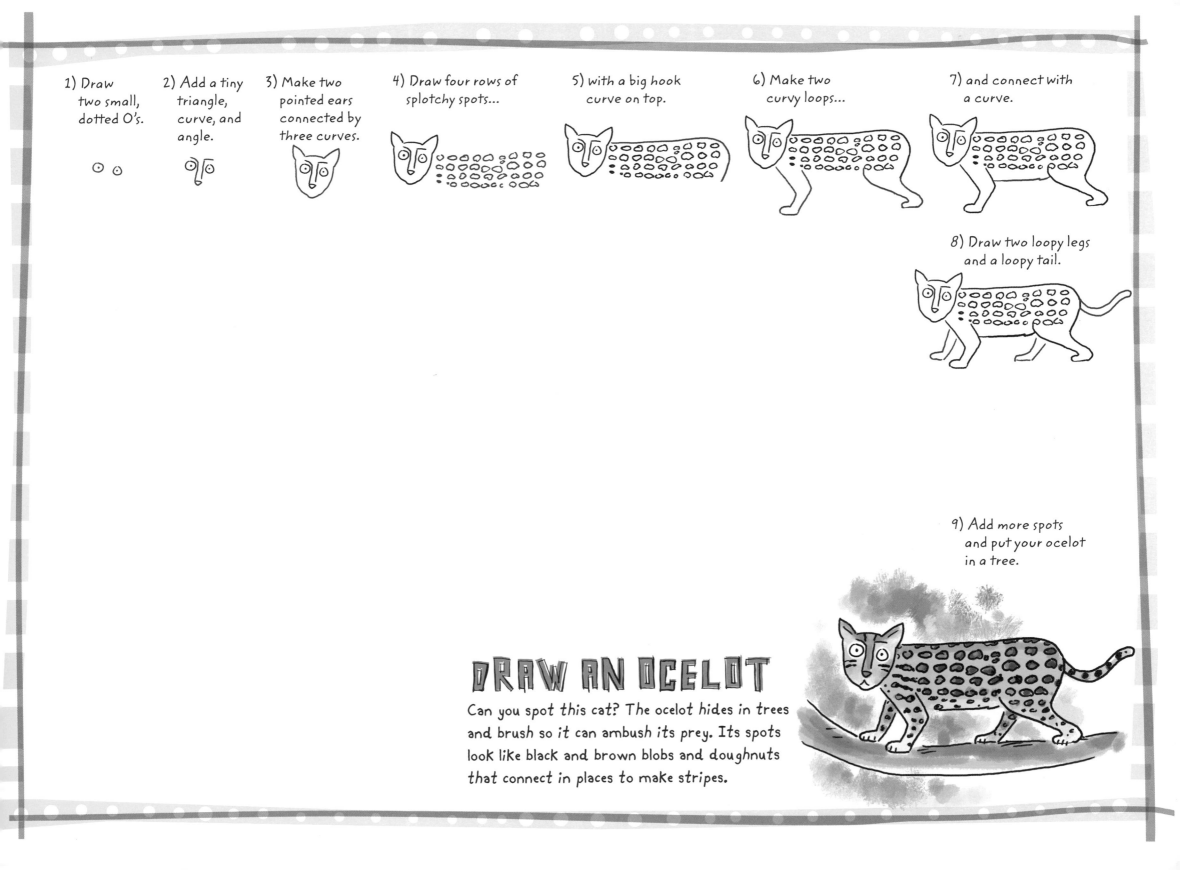

1) Draw a big P.

2) Add a curlicue.

3) Draw a wide P.

4) Add two curvy loops.

5) Draw five curves...

6) and four dainty feet.

DRAW A PIG

Why did the pig turn on the oven?
Because she was bacon!
People started raising pigs for food
thousands of years ago in Asia.

P is for People

It's fun to turn P's into people.

Start with a P and then...

put eyes on top...

or put the eyes inside...

or give your person glasses...

or make your person swing.

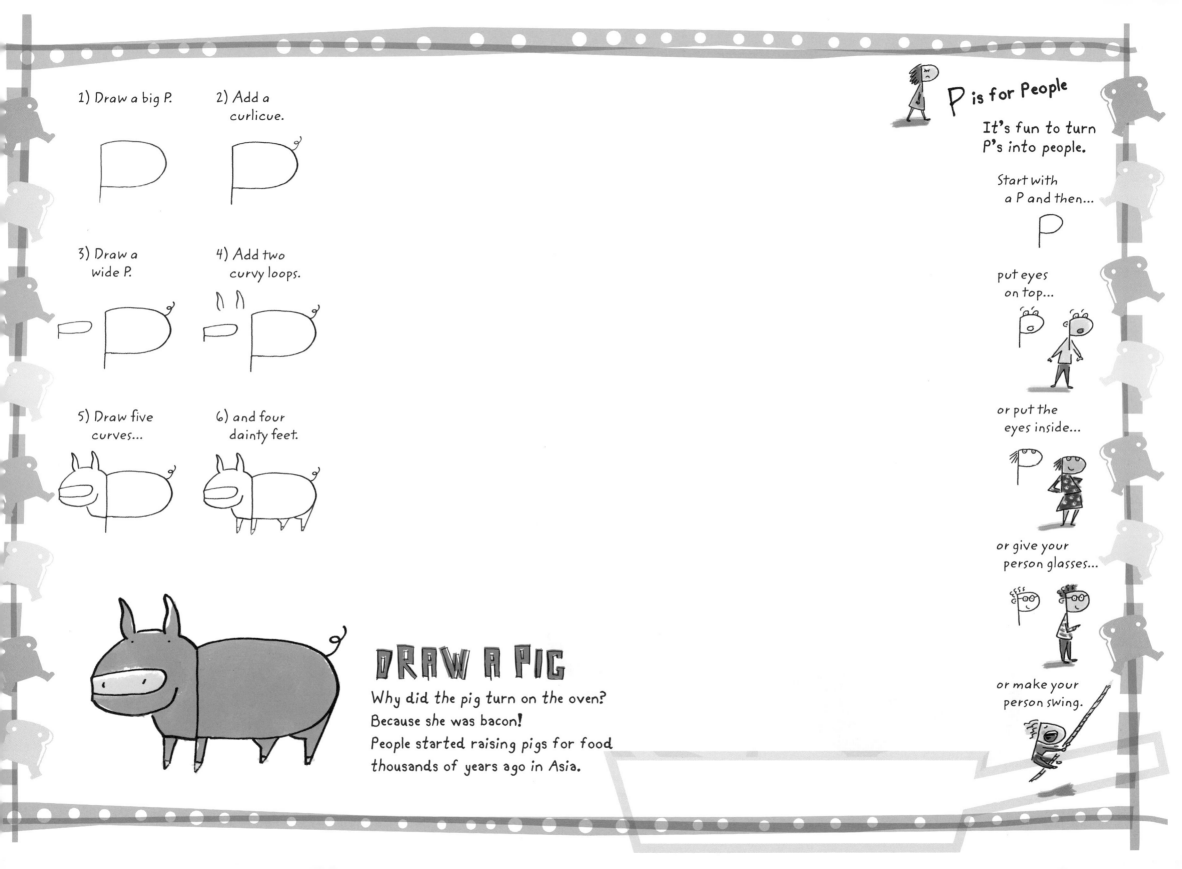

DRAW A QUETZAL

The quetzal is a colorful Central American bird with a very, very long tail.

1) Draw a q with a long tail.

2) Add three long curves...

3) four short green curves...

4) and seven more short curves.

5) Draw a leaning p...

6) connect a y...

7) and add a ziggy curve.

1) Draw an R.

2) Add a rounded angle...

3) and a curvy V.

4) Draw a squiggly ball...

5) two teardrops, a sideways V...

6) two dots, and a loopy paw.

DRAW A RABBIT

Rabbits are everywhere! They live on every continent except Antarctica.
Rabbits eat carrots and any other vegetation they can get their paws on,
and they eat a lot because their digestive systems work as quick as bunnies!

1) Draw a fat swoopy S.

2) Attach two striped curves.

3) Add loopy hands...

4) and a U.

5) Use five curves to draw a face.

6) Add a b lying down...

7) and two beans.

8) Add four swirl wheels and go!

DRAW A SKATEBOARDER

It's just a board with four wheels, but for the boarders who can flip, whirl, and hang upside down, skateboarding is like a magic carpet ride.

1) Draw a t.

2) Put a curve around the top...

3) and a box with a rounded top around that.

4) Add a big doughnut and a little doughnut...

5) and draw squiggle curves inside.

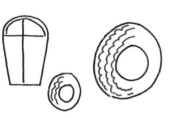

6) Attach two J's, one upside down, and one sideways.

7) Add a square C and a round C...

8) and five t's.

9) Make a steering wheel and seat.

DRAW A TRACTOR

That bowl of cereal is on your breakfast table thanks to the invention of the engine-powered farm tractor, which could pull a plow longer, faster, and stronger than a horse, mule, ox, or human.

1) Draw a u.   2) Add a skinny striped triangle...   3) and a small black triangle.   4) Attach a C...   5) and a striped slice.   6) Draw a wide u...   7) and a sideways S.   8) Add four tail S's...   9) and four V legs with wedge feet.

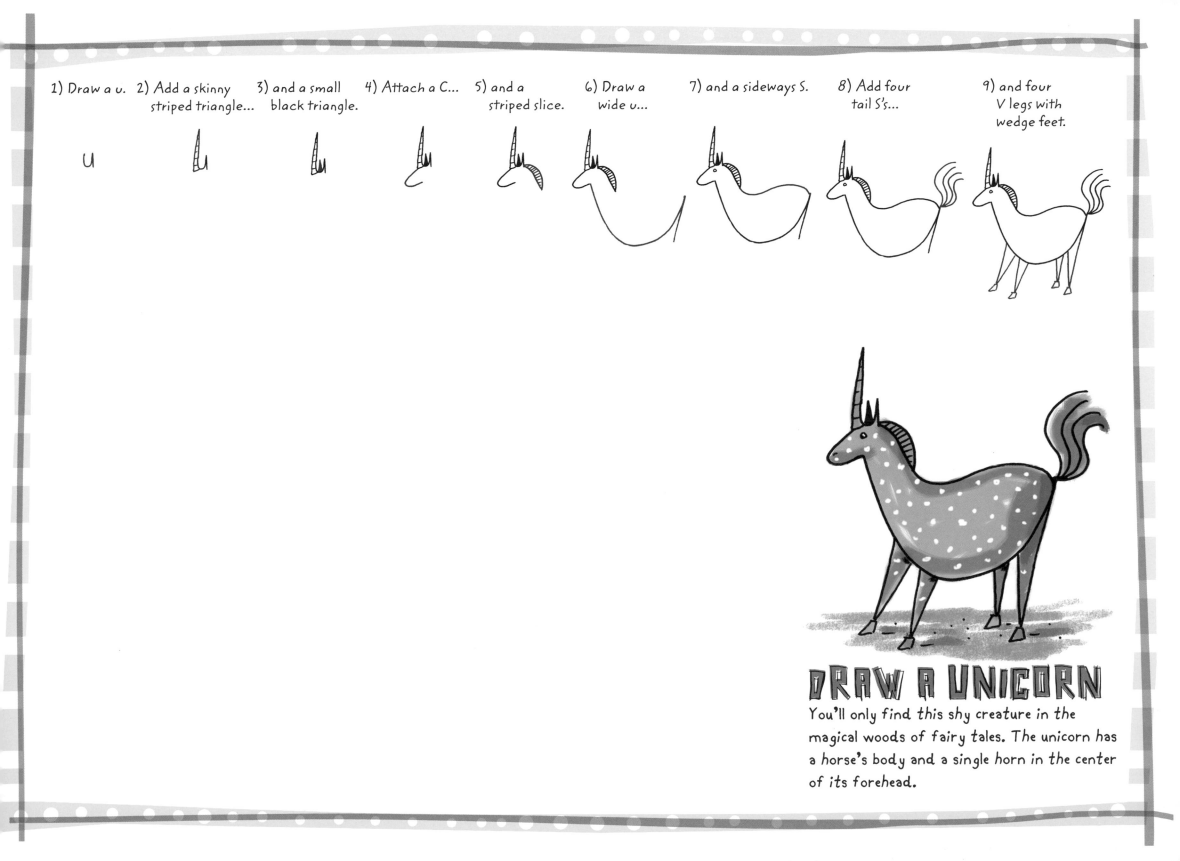

DRAW A UNICORN

You'll only find this shy creature in the magical woods of fairy tales. The unicorn has a horse's body and a single horn in the center of its forehead.

1) Draw a V.

2) Attach four more at the point.

3) Top with five curvy V's.

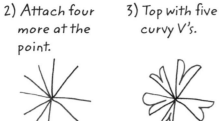

4) Put five hearts on top of those.

5) Add ziggy lines.

DRAW A VENUS FLYTRAP

Here's a plant with bad table manners. When an insect comes nearby, the leaves of the flytrap snap shut and hold the insect until it's been digested.

1) Draw a W with curvy tops.

2) Add two short curves and two long curves.

3) Make loopy hands.

4) Draw a face with d and b eyes.

5) Make a beard of 19 short curves.

6) Attach a big wedge.

7) Draw stars and swirls and cast a spell!

DRAW A WIZARD

Found in stories and myths from all over the world, wizards have magical powers. You can do magic, too, and turn the letter W into a mysterious sorcerer.

Switch to a witch.

Instead of a wizard, cast your spell on a W and doodle a witch.

1) Draw a slanted X.

2) Put a box on top...

3) and a skinny box to the side.

4) Make two rows of twelve lines from short to long...

5) and connect the ends.

6) Draw fourteen squared loops from short to long.

7) Draw part of another X underneath.

DRAW A XYLOPHONE

Xylophones may have been the first musical instruments ever made. They can be made of wood, metal, plastic bottles, even gourds— the shorter the bar, the higher the sound.

1) Draw a y.

2) Add a long horizontal line.

3) Add four more horizontal lines.

4) Draw sixteen short angled lines.

5) Add eleven portholes and eight windows.

6) Put radar on top...

7) and zip through the waves!

DRAW A YACHT

All aboard for a pleasure cruise!

1) Draw two Z's.

2) Connect the sides.

3) Draw a zigzag on top...

4) and put a 7 around it.

5) Add zigzag hair and beard...

6) four more Z's...

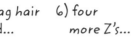

7) two arms and legs...

8) and zap! a lightning bolt.

DRAW ZEUS

Zeus is the king of gods in Greek mythology, and the master of thunder and lightning.

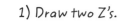

1) Draw an egg.

2) Attach two curves.

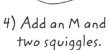

3) Put a loop inside.

4) Add an M and two squiggles.

5) Make an eye and two super squiggles...

6) and two V's on the bottom.

7) Draw loopy feet...

8) and color your chicken blue—or white—or brown. Chickens come in lots of colors!

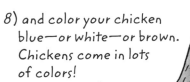

DRAW A CHICKEN

Which came first, the chicken or the egg? In this doodle, the egg is first!

Start by drawing an egg shape—an oval that's smaller at one end than the other.

1) Draw two eggs.

2) Make a curvy V.

3) Attach two overlapping V's.

4) Connect top and bottom with curves.

5) Add legs and feet...

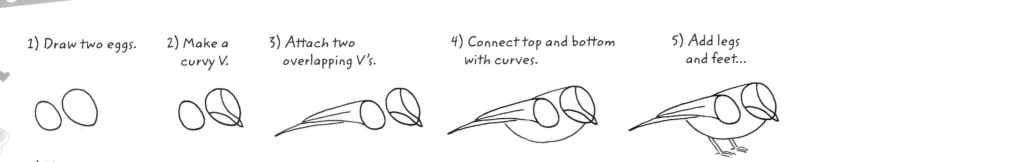

6) black cap, and bib!

DRAW A BLACK-CAPPED CHICKADEE

This little bird always wears a black cap—and a bib. Both stay on, even when the chickadee hangs upside down from a tree branch looking for food.

1) Draw an egg.

2) Attach two curves...

3) and two V's.

4) Attach nine loopy feathers to one V...

5) and eleven loopy feathers to the other.

6) Make seven loopy tail feathers...

7) two V feet, an eye, a beak...

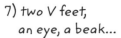

8) and fly!

DRAW A ROBIN

The early bird catches the worm—and then lays an egg. Unlike most birds, who lay their eggs at dawn, robins lay their blue eggs in the middle of the morning after they've eaten.

DRAW AN EMU

An emu egg is EGGSTRA large. Its yolk is the size of a doughnut, and one scrambled emu egg is enough to feed five people.

Actual size!
→

1) Draw a squiggly egg.

2) Attach two squiggly V's to each end.

3) Add five squiggly curves.

4) Put a little egg with a V attached on top.

5) Draw four lines...

6) and attach loopy feet.

1) Draw most of an egg.

2) Add a squiggly line across the top...

3) and two squiggly lines coming out.

4) Draw most of another egg.

5) Add two curvy lines coming out.

DRAW A CROCODILE

Let me out of here! A crocodile is born with a mouthful of very sharp teeth, but it uses a tiny one on its snout called the eggtooth to break out of its shell.

1) Draw a frog egg.

2) Add two curvy stripes.

3) Make a curvy 7...

4) and attach a curvy curve.

5) Draw two loops...

6) and attach two feet with loopy toes.

7) Add lots of blobs and wait; what's that flying by?

8) Time for breakfast!

DRAW A LEOPARD FROG

Don't reach across the table for your food—unless you're a frog!

1) Start with a tiny round fish egg.

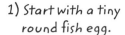

2) Attach two curves on either side.

3) Add a little egg eye and three curves.

4) Draw eight curves on one side and five on the other.

5) Put eight more curves on the end.

6) Add a bunch of bubbles.

DRAW A SIAMESE FIGHTING FISH

This daddy is a fighter and a father. The male Siamese fighting fish makes a nest of bubbles, carries each egg to the nest, and then cares for the eggs until they hatch and start to swim.

1) Draw a striped egg.

2) Add a squiggly O on top...

3) and a loop on top of that.

4) Make four curves...

5) six angles...

6) and two loop wings.

7) Draw six-sided shapes to make a royal honeycomb.

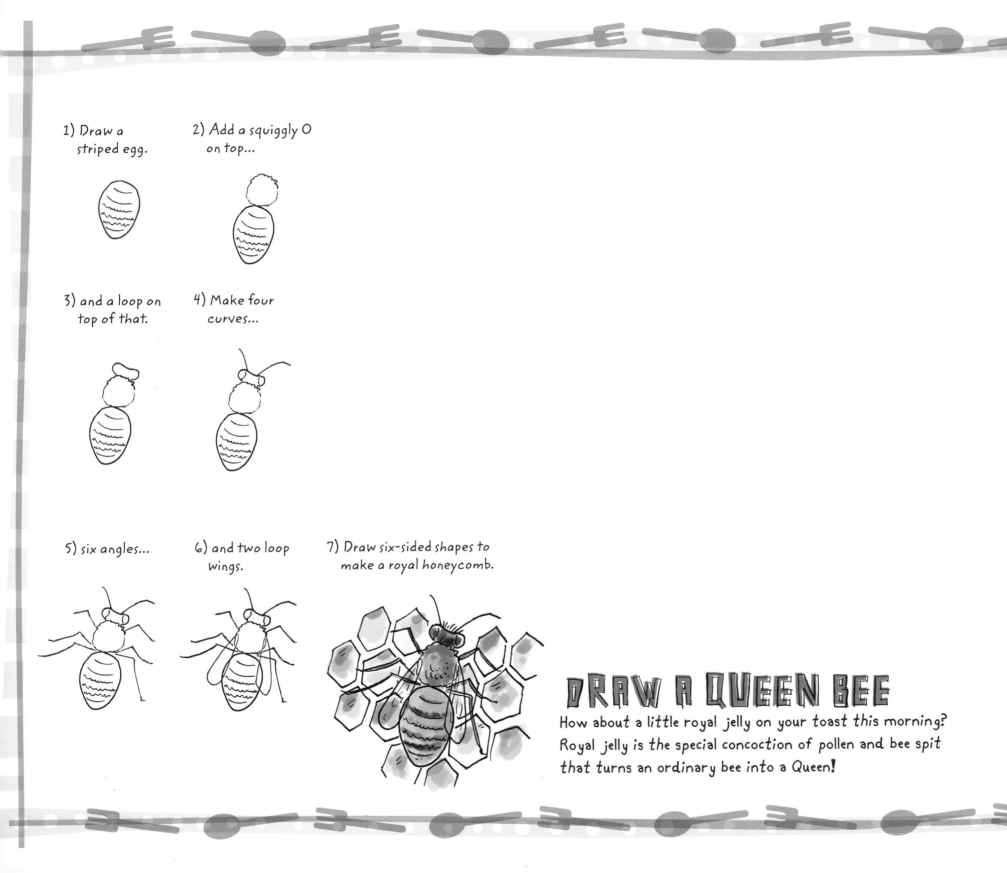

DRAW A QUEEN BEE

How about a little royal jelly on your toast this morning? Royal jelly is the special concoction of pollen and bee spit that turns an ordinary bee into a Queen!

1) Draw an egg.

2) Attach a curvy V to one end.

3) Add six curves at the other end.

4) Make a loop with a squiggly end.

5) Add four ziggy feet, each with webbed toes.

6) Draw two eyes and two nostrils that can open and close.

7) Make fur out of rows of curved lines.

8) Throw your platypus in the water to swim!

DRAW A PLATYPUS

The platypus may be *the weirdest animal in the world*. It lays eggs, but *it's* a mammal. It has a snout like a duck with nostrils that close when *it* goes underwater. It has fur like an otter and webbed feet to swim, but at the end of each toe is a claw to dig.

1) Draw an egg.

2) Put a bowtie in the middle.

3) Make a V around it.

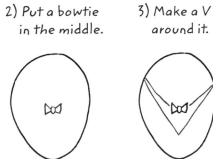

4) Draw a face...

5) and two bent arms and legs.

6) Make loopy hands and shoes...

7) and a fancy coat and hat.

8) Put Mr. Dumpty sitting at the top!

DRAW HUMPTY DUMPTY

The world's most famous egg was sitting high until...!

1) Draw an egg.

2) Attach two curves.

3) Put a loop inside.

4) Add an M and two squiggles.

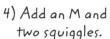

5) Make an eye and two super squiggles...

6) and two V's on the bottom.

7) Draw loopy feet...

8) and color your chicken blue—or white—or brown. Chickens come in lots of colors!

DRAW A CHICKEN

Which came first, the chicken or the egg? In this doodle, the egg is first! Start by drawing an egg shape—an oval that's smaller at one end than the other.